MULTIPLE TRADING POSITION STRATEGY

USD-M & COIN-M Futures Contract in Binance

Crypto Space - 2024

CONTENTS

Title Page
Introduction

INTRODUCTION

This strategy will guide you to manage your trading through opening multiple trading position. We will divide our funds into two division to to trade in Usdm and CoinM Futures Contract in Binance. With this, you can maximize your profit in Spot and Futures Trading. This is one of the strategy that i like because of its low risk potential.

SETTING FIRST YOUR BINANCE ACCOUNT

1. You must have a verified binance account.
2. Make sure your account is in hedge mode. Follow the Step by Step Screenshot below to set it up.

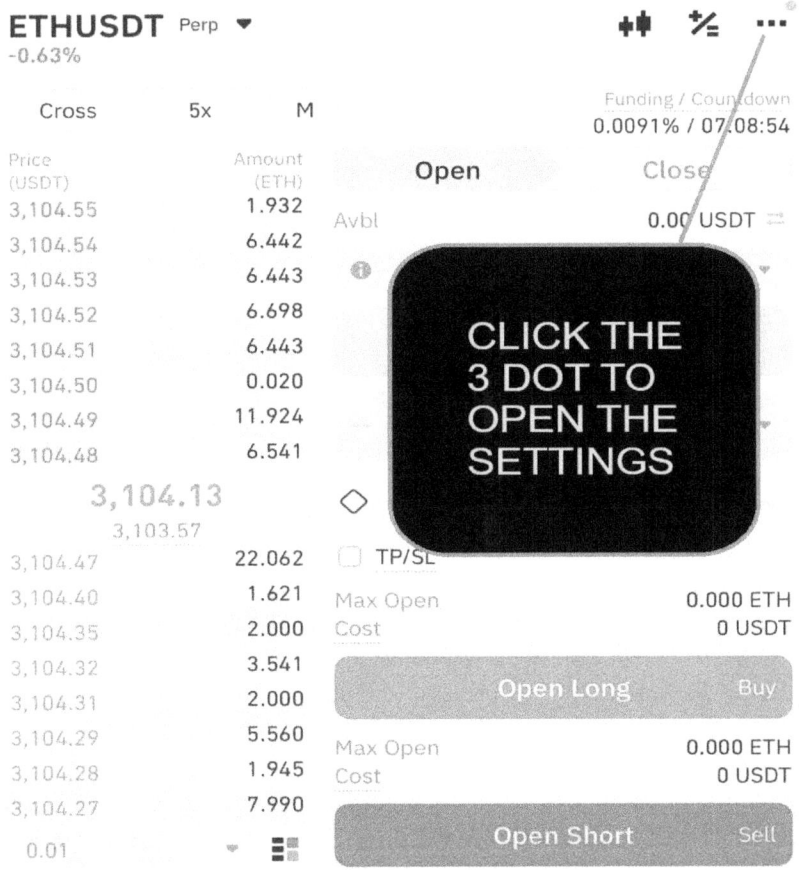

3. Click the preferences:

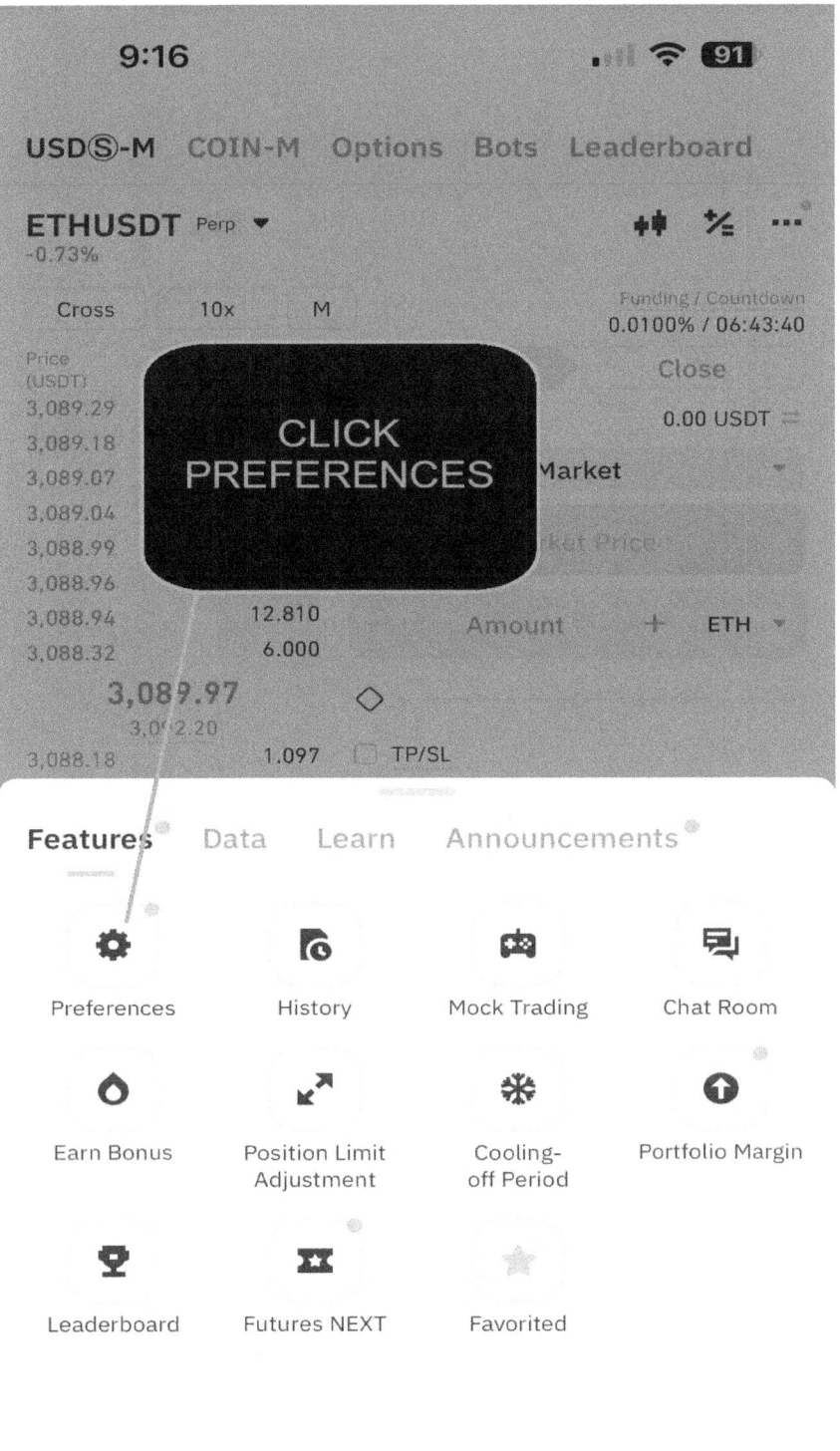

4. Click and select "HEDGE MODE"

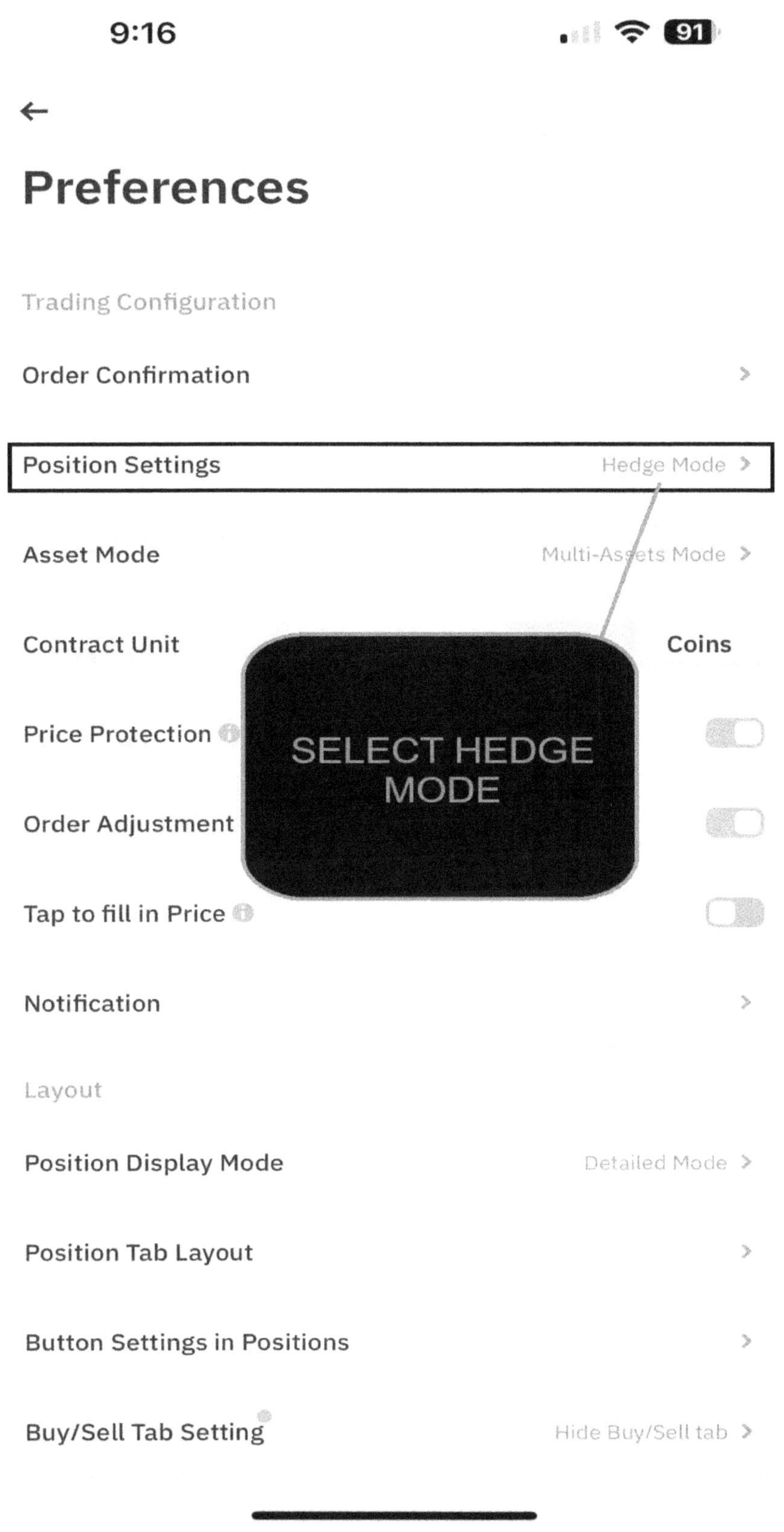

9:16

←

Preferences

Trading Configuration

Order Confirmation >

| Position Settings   Hedge Mode > |

Asset Mode   Multi-Assets Mode >

Contract Unit   Coins

Price Protection ⓘ

SELECT HEDGE MODE

Order Adjustment

Tap to fill in Price ⓘ

Notification >

Layout

Position Display Mode   Detailed Mode >

Position Tab Layout >

Button Settings in Positions >

Buy/Sell Tab Setting   Hide Buy/Sell tab >

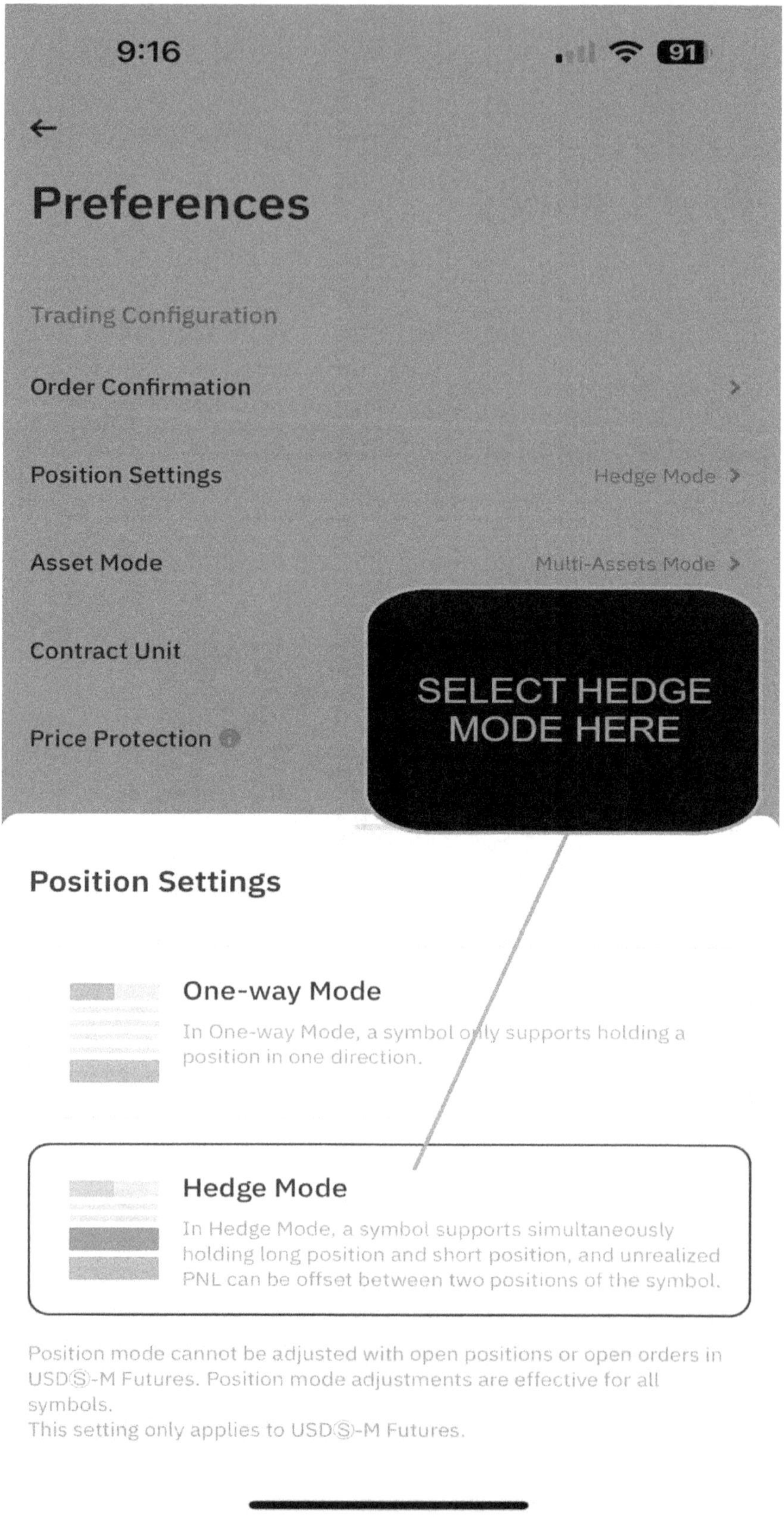

Preferences

Trading Configuration

Order Confirmation >

Position Settings Hedge Mode >

Asset Mode Multi-Assets Mode >

Contract Unit

Price Protection

SELECT HEDGE MODE HERE

Position Settings

 **One-way Mode**
In One-way Mode, a symbol only supports holding a position in one direction.

 **Hedge Mode**
In Hedge Mode, a symbol supports simultaneously holding long position and short position, and unrealized PNL can be offset between two positions of the symbol.

Position mode cannot be adjusted with open positions or open orders in USDⓈ-M Futures. Position mode adjustments are effective for all symbols.
This setting only applies to USDⓈ-M Futures.

Deposit Funds in Binance

1. Go to "home" and click "Deposit".

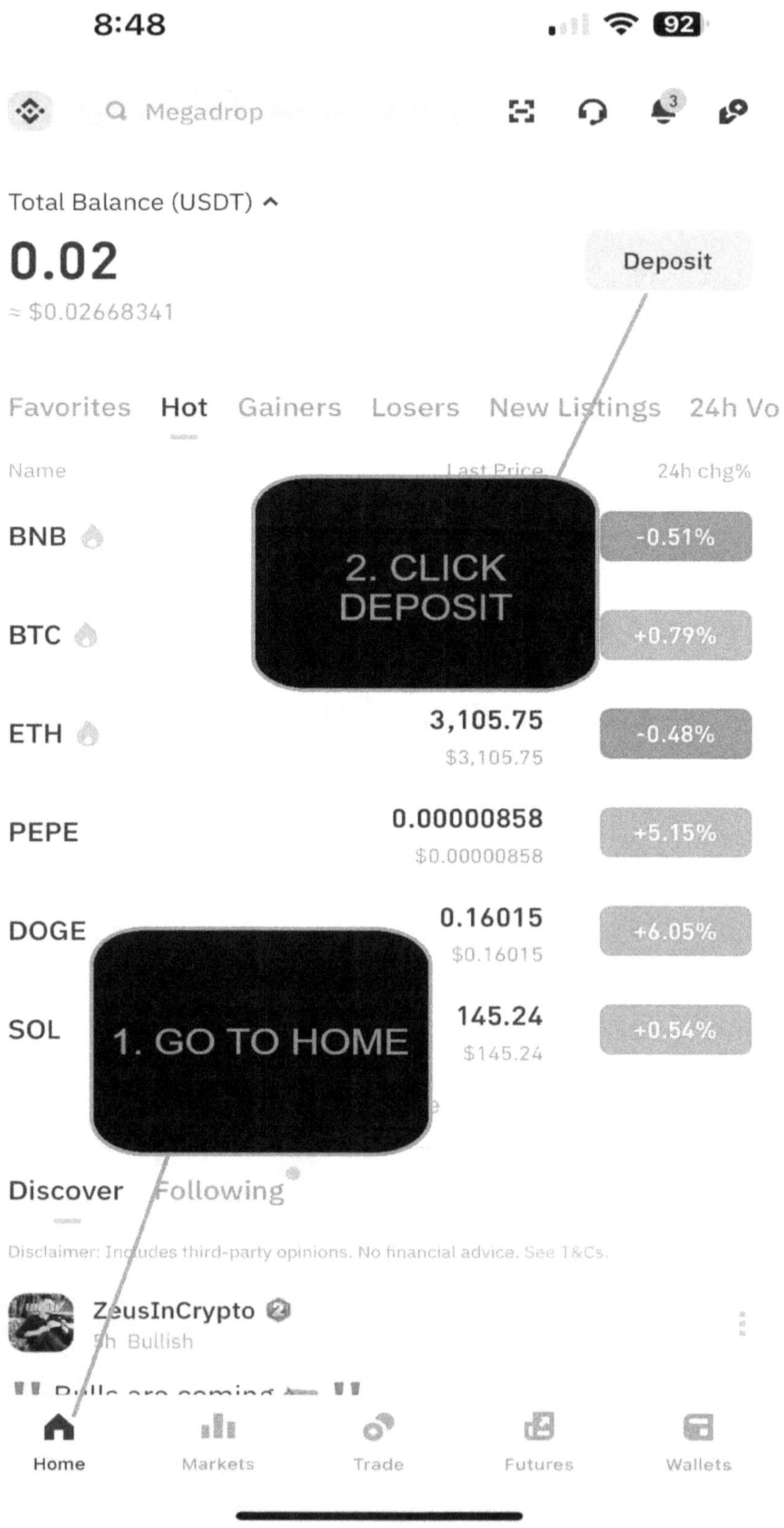

8:48

Megadrop

Total Balance (USDT)

0.02

≈ $0.02668341

Deposit

Favorites **Hot** Gainers Losers New Listings 24h Vo

Name	Last Price	24h chg%
BNB		-0.51%
BTC		+0.79%
ETH	3,105.75 $3,105.75	-0.48%
PEPE	0.00000858 $0.00000858	+5.15%
DOGE	0.16015 $0.16015	+6.05%
SOL	145.24 $145.24	+0.54%

2. CLICK DEPOSIT

1. GO TO HOME

Discover Following

Disclaimer: Includes third-party opinions. No financial advice. See T&Cs.

ZeusInCrypto
5h Bullish

Home Markets Trade Futures Wallets

2. Select "P2P Trading"

Deposit

I don't have crypto assets

Recommend

 P2P Trading
Bank Transfer, Digital Wallet Transfer, Mobile Payment and...

 Deposit PHP
Multiple payment options

 Buy with PHP
Embrace the variety of payment methods!

I have

SELECT P2P TRADING

3. Tap on "P2P"

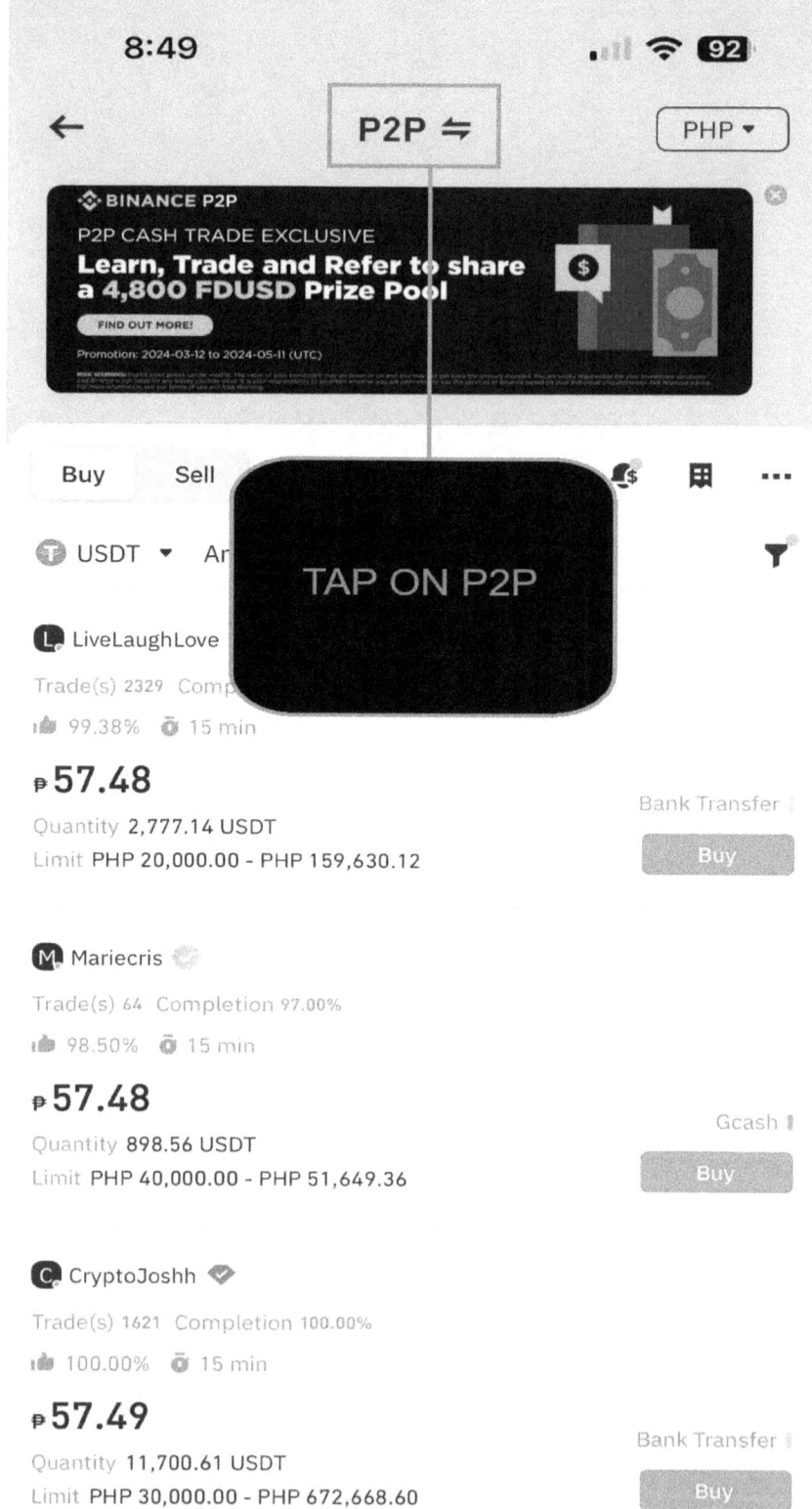

4. Tap on "EXPRESS"

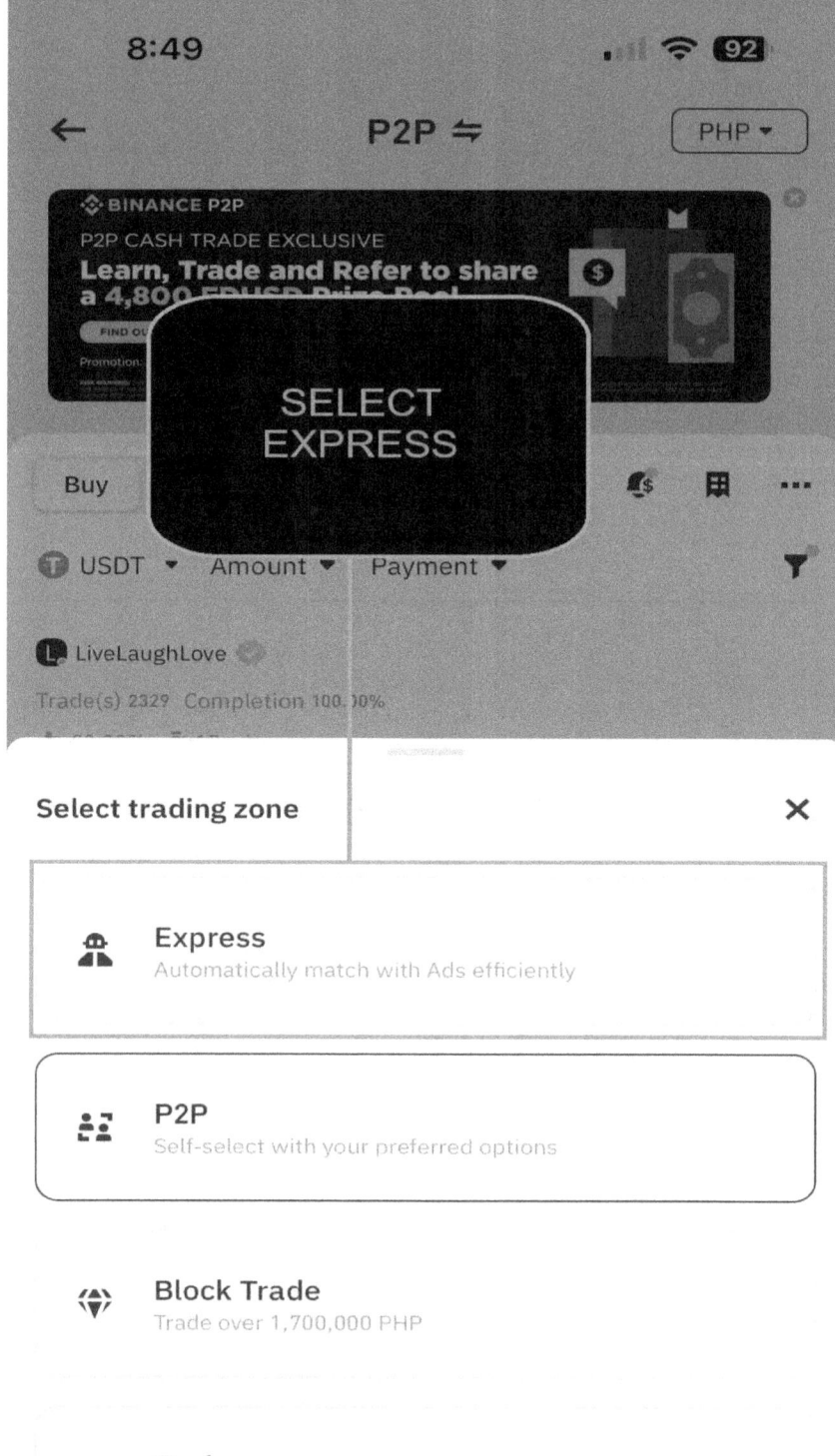

SELECT EXPRESS

Select trading zone ✕

Express
Automatically match with Ads efficiently

P2P
Self-select with your preferred options

Block Trade
Trade over 1,700,000 PHP

Cash
Trade crypto in person via cash

5. Put your desired amount of funds in the "Box" that you want to deposit then connect and transact with anyone who is selling USDT by clicking "Buy USDT" (This part is very straight forward).

Divisions of Coin

The importance about this strategy is actually doesn't require a lot of Technical Analysis to enter a trade. Most of the traders only choose to play "Spot Trading" or "Futures Trading". But here, we will be considering this two kinds of trading to maximize of potential profit in the future.

We will be dividing our funds into two. For the first division is for USD-M Futures and the second division is COIN-M Futures. The essence of this strategy is even you are only trading with one coin their is what we called sub-division for a specific coin. Example Ethereum coin below:

USD-M FUTURES (DIVISION 1)
- ETHUSDT (Perp)
- ETHUSDT (Qtly 0628)
- ETHUSDT (Qtly 0927)

COIN-M FUTURES (DIVISION 2)
- ETHUSD CM (Perp)
- ETHUSD CM (Qtly 0628)
- ETHUSD CM (Qtly 0927)

In this option of sub-division for Ethereum, for the first one which is "Perp" means perpetual (This one is no expiration) but for the "Qtly" means quarterly which has an expiration. So make sure to exit any position or trade with a "Qtly" Sub-division before the expiration.

USD-M FUTURES (DIVISION 1)

In this division, we are trading USDT here.

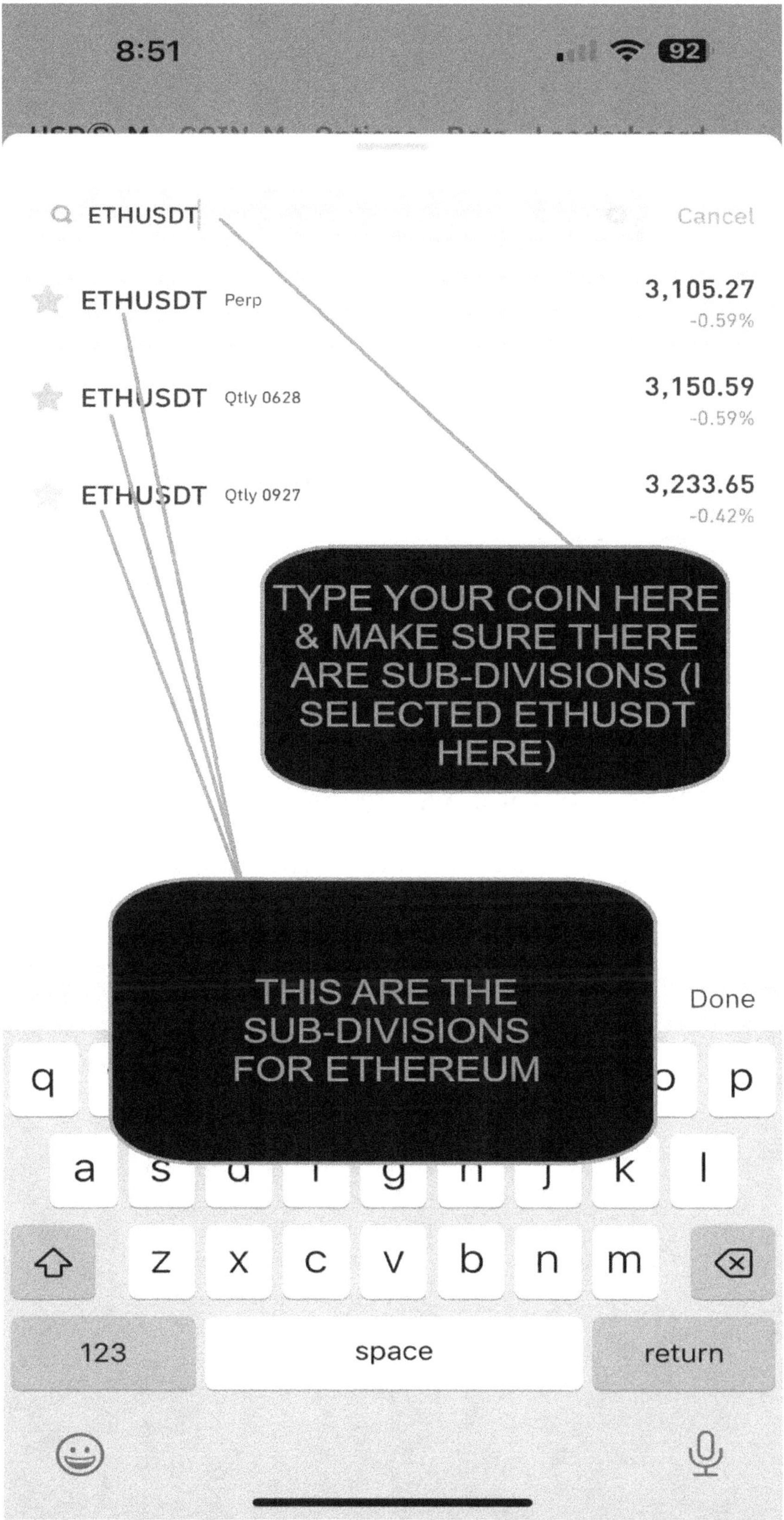
8:51
92
ETHUSDT
Cancel
ETHUSDT Perp
3,105.27
-0.59%
ETHUSDT Qtly 0628
3,150.59
-0.59%
ETHUSDT Qtly 0927
3,233.65
-0.42%
TYPE YOUR COIN HERE & MAKE SURE THERE ARE SUB-DIVISIONS (I SELECTED ETHUSDT HERE)
THIS ARE THE SUB-DIVISIONS FOR ETHEREUM
Done

COIN-M FUTURES (DIVISION 2)

In this division, we are trading Spot coin.

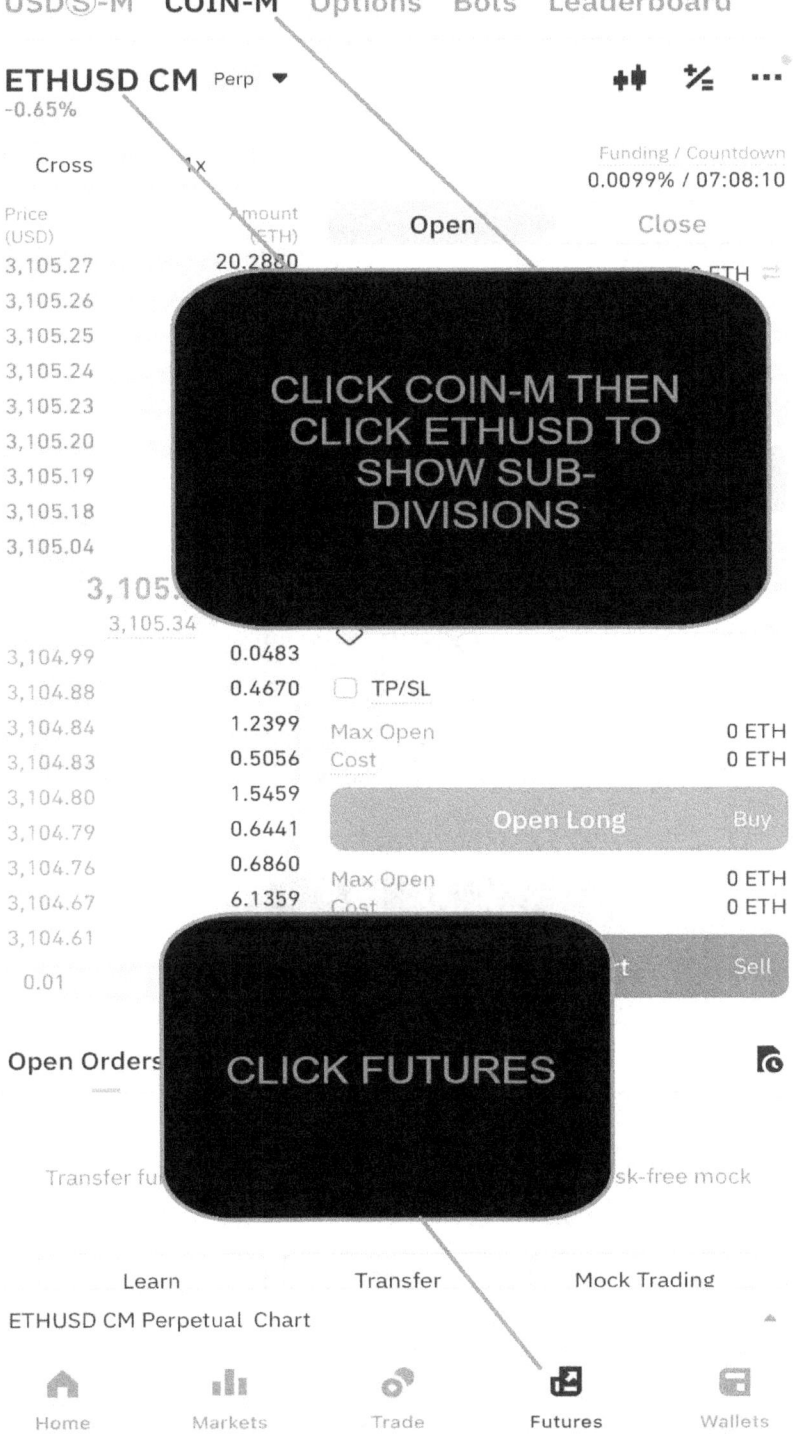

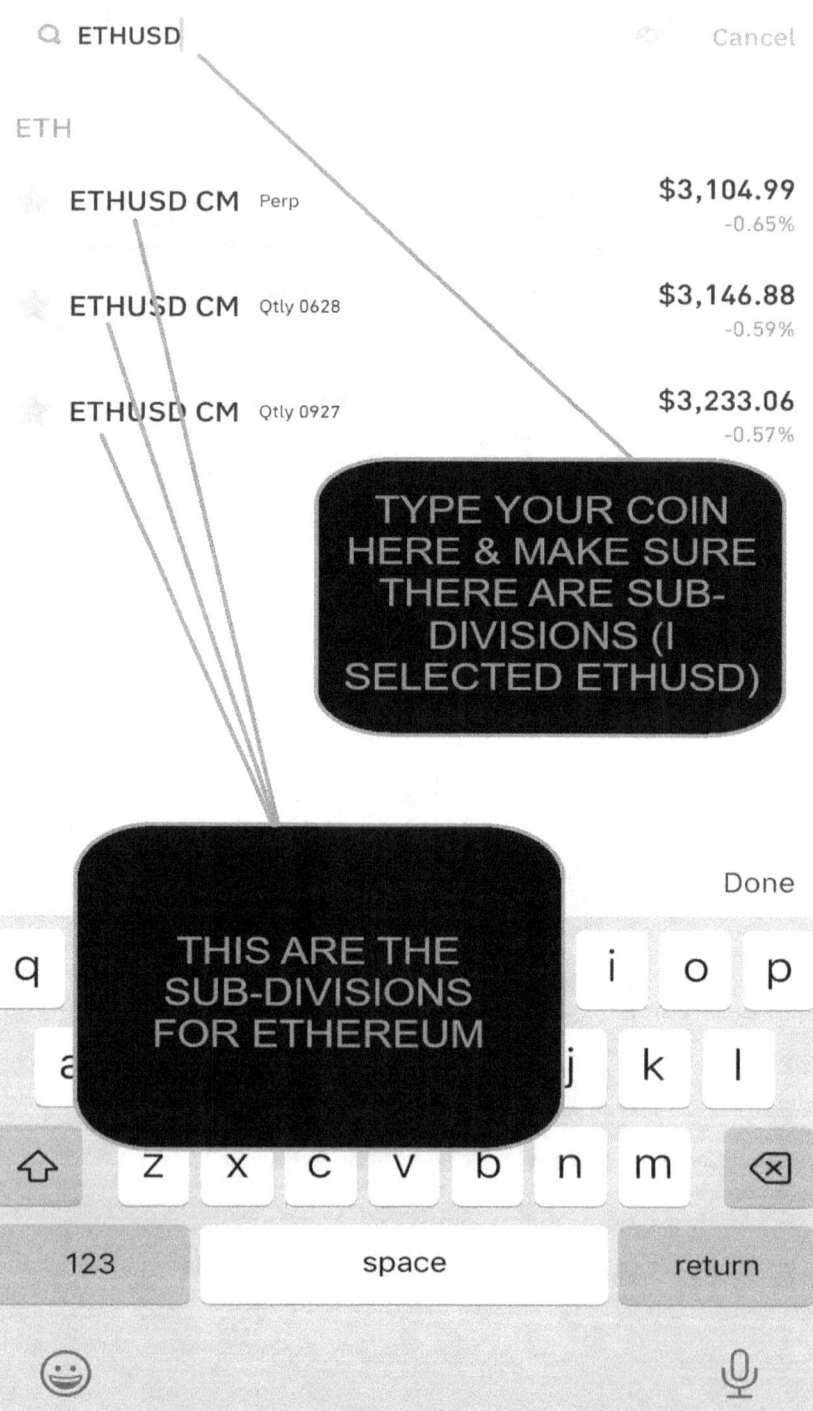

Settings for "Margin Mode" and "Leverage"

For this settings, it applies to both divisions (USD-M and COIN-M).
Margin Mode: Cross / Leverage: 10x

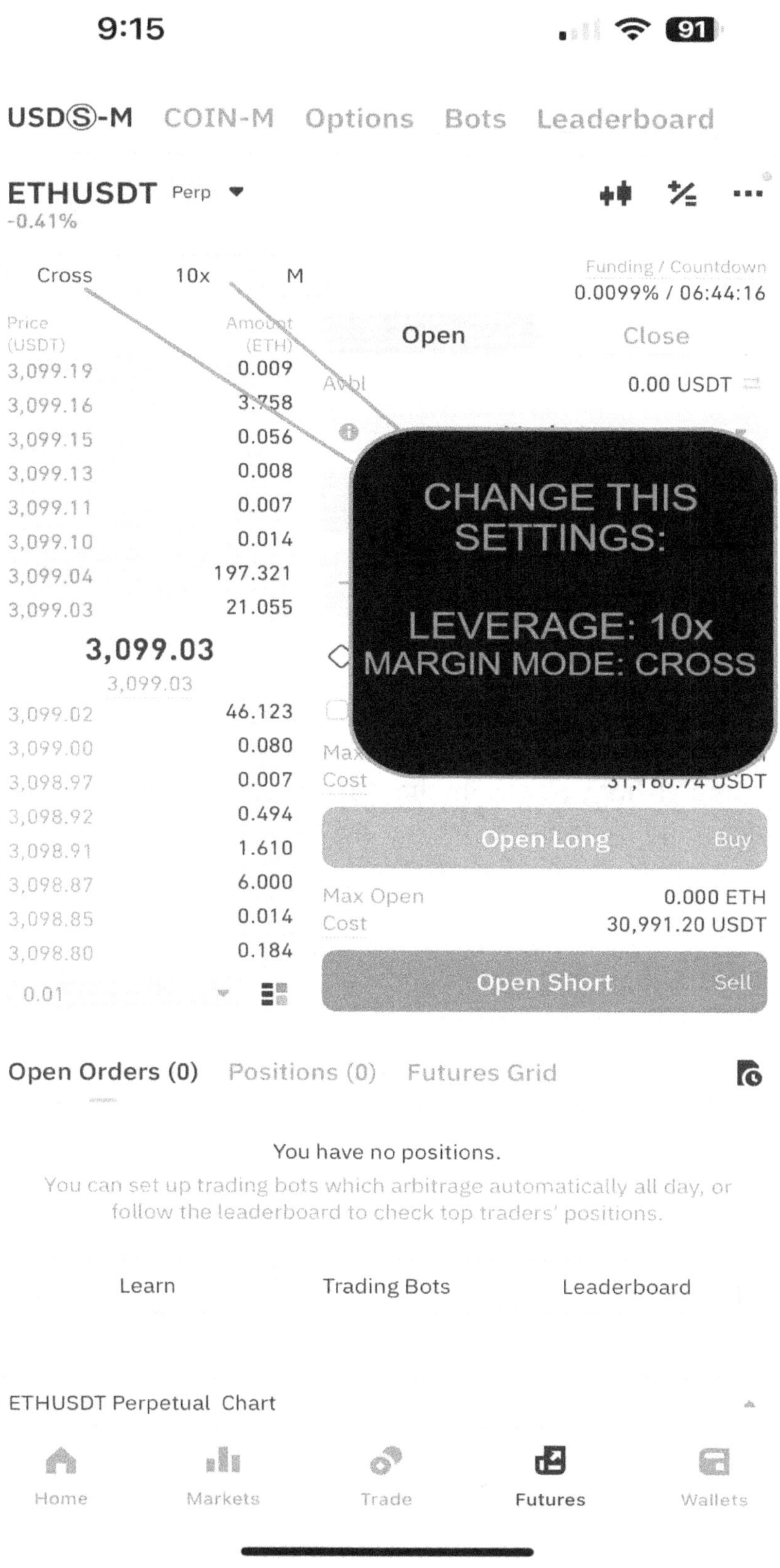

9:15

USD(S)-M COIN-M Options Bots Leaderboard

ETHUSDT Perp ▼
-0.41%

Cross   10x   M

Funding / Countdown
0.0099% / 06:44:16

Price (USDT)	Amount (ETH)
3,099.19	0.009
3,099.16	3.758
3,099.15	0.056
3,099.13	0.008
3,099.11	0.007
3,099.10	0.014
3,099.04	197.321
3,099.03	21.055

3,099.03
3,099.03

3,099.02	46.123
3,099.00	0.080
3,098.97	0.007
3,098.92	0.494
3,098.91	1.610
3,098.87	6.000
3,098.85	0.014
3,098.80	0.184

0.01 ▼

Open   **Close**

Avbl   0.00 USDT

> **CHANGE THIS SETTINGS:**
>
> **LEVERAGE: 10x**
> **MARGIN MODE: CROSS**

Max Open
Cost   31,180.74 USDT

Open Long   Buy

Max Open   0.000 ETH
Cost   30,991.20 USDT

Open Short   Sell

Open Orders (0)   Positions (0)   Futures Grid

You have no positions.
You can set up trading bots which arbitrage automatically all day, or follow the leaderboard to check top traders' positions.

Learn   Trading Bots   Leaderboard

ETHUSDT Perpetual Chart

 Home   Markets   Trade   **Futures**   Wallets

Funds Computation per Division

Now, before we proceed with the actual trading, how are we going to manage our funds to enter a trade? First, we need to divide the funds as we mention it earlier. Below are the percentage per Division:

If i deposited **400 usdt** in my account,

1st Division - 25% of USD-M
2nd Division - 75% of COIN-M

For the 1st Division, 25% of 400 usdt is 100 usdt. So, we need to put 100 usdt in our USDM-M wallet. Since, we need usdt to trade in USD-M Futures.

For the 2nd Division, 75% of 400 usdt is 300 usdt. This remaining 75% must be in the spot wallet, we will be using this funds to buy the coin in "Spot Trading".After you bought the coin, go to COIN-M Futures to transfer the coin from Spot. Since, we need coin to trade in COIN-M Futures.

Buying Coin in Spot Trading

Go to "Spot Trading" then click Eth / USDT (you can select any coin here as long as it has a sub-divisions)

Executing the Actual Trade

Now, that all funds are in respective divisions (USDM-M & COIN-M) based on percentage. Always keep in your mind to follow every step and procedure. The idea of this strategy is to minimize or to have a no liquidation for every positions or trades that you open and also to stay in the market even your trade is against the trend.

For example, we started a long or buy trade and just buy the coin in market price. So, we will be considering a set profit of 2% to 5% because this percentage is very attainable for a specific coin. **"If our trade is against the market trend** and it reaches to negative 100%, we will be opening the next sub-division. Below are the arrangement for opening orders for every Sub-divisions after reaching a negative 100%.

USD-M FUTURES (DIVISION 1)
ETHUSDT (Perp)

ETHUSDT (Qtly 0628)
- after ETHUSDT (Perp) reaching negative 100%, you should open this Sub-Division ETHUSDT (Qtly 0628)

ETHUSDT (Qtly 0927)
- after ETHUSDT (Qtly 0628) reaching negative 100% again, you should open this Sub-Division ETHUSDT (Qtly 0927)

Now, if all the Sub-Divisions in USD-M Futures are in negative, we switch to COIN-M Futures

COIN-M FUTURES (DIVISION 2)

ETHUSD CM (Perp)
- after ETHUSDT (Qtly 0927) reaching negative 100%, you should open this Sub-Division ETHUSD CM (Perp)

ETHUSD CM (Qtly 0628)

- after ETHUSD CM (Perp) reaching negative 100%, you should open this Sub-Division ETHUSD CM (Qtly 0628)

ETHUSD CM (Qtly 0927)
- after ETHUSD CM (Qtly 0628) reaching negative 100%, you should open this Sub-Division ETHUSD CM (Qtly 0927)

Take Note:
Not all Sub-Divisions will be opened. This scenario is to far to happen. Just to explain the sequence of the strategy. Because always remember, whatever comes down always comes up. So, even if you have a negative Sub-divisions, if the market trend will be in favor with your open trades, say for example you reached and opened all the three sub-divisions in the USD-M Futures, all of negative profit will turn green in the future. The funds are still there. Thats the good thing about this strategy, no matter how many trades you open in the Sub-divisions, if you follow the procedure accordingly, you will stay unliquidated and continue the trade.

You can have a good profit even without using all the Sub-divisions that are mentioned. If by chance, you used all the Sub-divisions, add some funds in your account to stay un-liquidated. Always read the procedure over and over again to master it.

Placing Amount in USD-M & COIN-M

Same amount will be place in USD-M and COIN-M. Every trade open, place an amount of **100 Eth** based in the percentage amount of USD-M. So, our example is 400 usdt and 25% of it is 100 usdt. So thats the basis for every trade you open. Put 100 in the amount. This will change based in your deposited funds. Get the 25% of your funds, that is the amount of your every trade position. If you choose bitcoin, put **100 btc** in the amount.

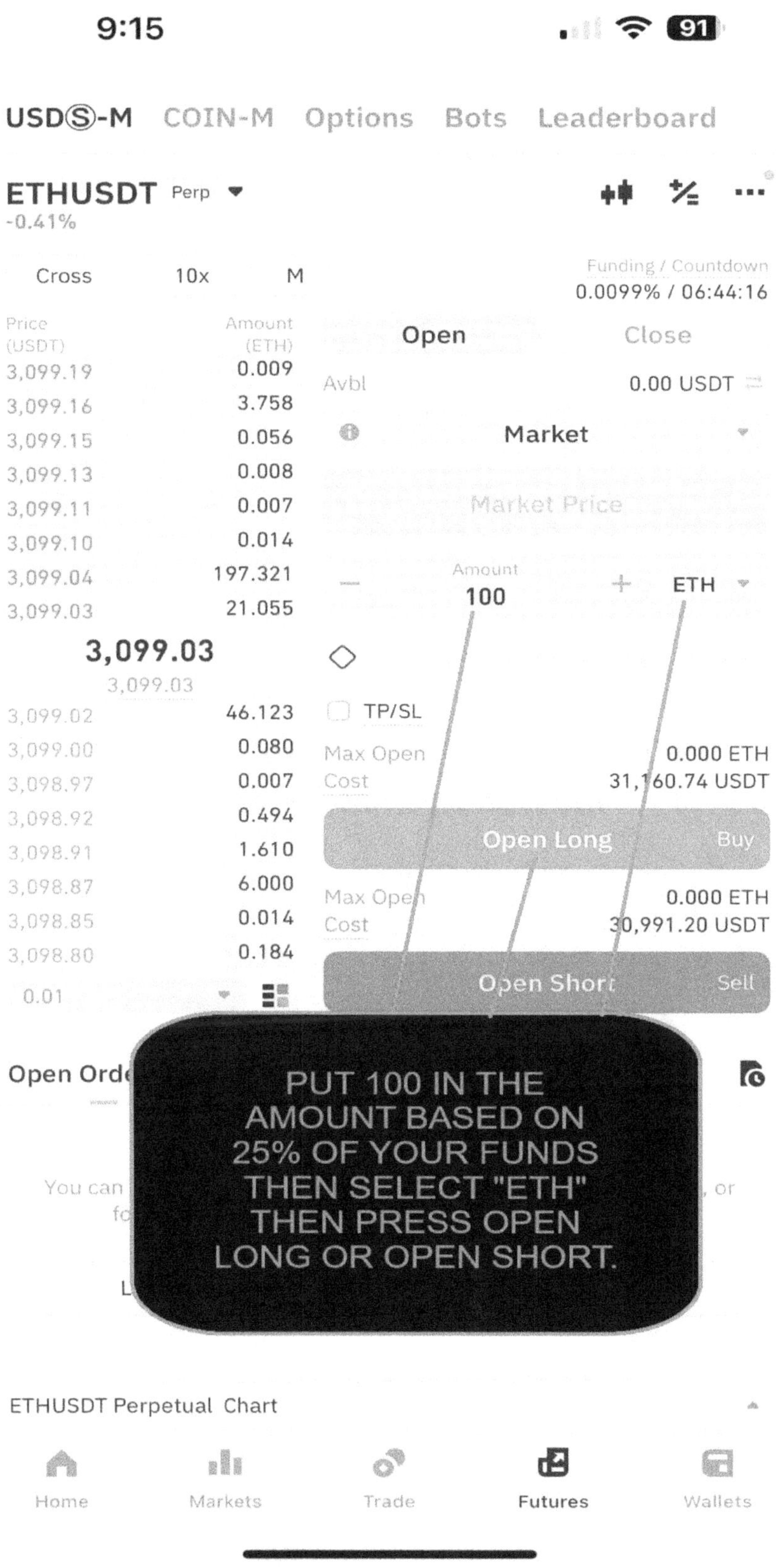

9:15

USDⓈ-M   COIN-M   Options   Bots   Leaderboard

ETHUSDT Perp ▼
-0.41%

Cross   10x   M

Funding / Countdown
0.0099% / 06:44:16

Price (USDT)	Amount (ETH)
3,099.19	0.009
3,099.16	3.758
3,099.15	0.056
3,099.13	0.008
3,099.11	0.007
3,099.10	0.014
3,099.04	197.321
3,099.03	21.055

3,099.03
3,099.03

3,099.02	46.123
3,099.00	0.080
3,098.97	0.007
3,098.92	0.494
3,098.91	1.610
3,098.87	6.000
3,098.85	0.014
3,098.80	0.184

0.01

Open   **Close**

Avbl   0.00 USDT

Market ▼

Market Price

— Amount +   ETH ▼
   100

◇
☐ TP/SL

Max Open   0.000 ETH
Cost   31,160.74 USDT

Open Long   Buy

Max Open   0.000 ETH
Cost   30,991.20 USDT

Open Short   Sell

Open Orders

> **PUT 100 IN THE AMOUNT BASED ON 25% OF YOUR FUNDS THEN SELECT "ETH" THEN PRESS OPEN LONG OR OPEN SHORT.**

ETHUSDT Perpetual Chart

 Home   Markets   Trade   **Futures**   Wallets

Always read the step by step over and over again to master it. Happy trade!

www.ingramcontent.com/pod-product-compliance
Lightning Source LLC
Chambersburg PA
CBHW050251230526
45470CB00005B/2212